Big Tools

for

Young Thinkers

Big Tools

for

Young Thinkers

Using Creative Problem Solving
Tools with Primary Students

Susan Keller-Mathers • *Kristin Puccio*

Published in cooperation with
Center for Creative Learning, Inc.

ISBN 1-882664-60-4

PRUFROCK PRESS
P.O. Box 8813
Waco, TX 76714-8813
Phone: (800) 998-2208
Fax: (800) 240-0333
www.prufrock.com

To our families—Gordon, Chris, and Rebecca Mathers; and Gerard and Gabriel Puccio, who provided us with the inspiration, love, and time to complete this book.

CONTENTS

INTRODUCTION

Big Tools for Young Thinkers presents eight tools to help primary students generate and evaluate ideas more effectively. The tools presented in this book have been successfully applied with both adults and children for over four decades. For the last seven years, we have worked in our primary classrooms to research and develop the adaptations for primary students presented in this tool book.

Big Tools Work Well for Small People

Responding to unique characteristics of your children, this book uses simplified language, manipulatives, visuals and symbols, and movement to help students understand and apply the tools.

So What's in This Book?

The first two lessons in this book are designed to introduce the rules for generating and focusing. Next, we present four generating and four focusing tools. There are two lessons for each tool. After the two lessons for each tool, we provide some helpful guidelines for going beyond an introduction to the tool. These will help you apply the tool to any problem solving situation of your choosing.

Each tool lesson is divided into seven sections. The first is the Purpose. The Purpose section describes the goal of the lesson. Next is the Key Point, which describes what the teacher should focus on for the lesson. The Materials and Preparation section lists all the materials needed to successfully do the lesson and any preparation necessary prior to the lesson. The next three sections are the steps to take to complete each lesson. The Warm Up provides an activity to draw the children into the lesson. It is used as a motivator. The section titled Digging Deeper describes steps to be taken that focus on the purpose of the lesson. The Extension section includes an opportunity to share work and debrief the children's learning from the lesson. The Enhancements section provides several ideas to help extend the lesson into other curriculum areas, or to extend the learning about CPS. The lessons are intended to be used independently and can be used in any order.

Summary of Tool Lessons

Generating and Focusing Rules Lessons

Lesson 1—Generating Rules. The purpose of this lesson is to help students understand the four guidelines followed when generating options. Follow these guidelines anytime you diverge or generate options using the tools of creative problem solving. By illustrating each rule and seeing a variety of other ways to represent the rules, students gain more insight into the meaning of the rule prior to using it to generate options.

Lesson 2—Focusing Rules. The purpose of this lesson is to help students understand the four guidelines for focusing options. These guidelines apply whenever you evaluate, refine, and develop options using the tools of creative problem solving presented in this book. By illustrating each rule and seeing a variety of other ways to represent the rules, students gain more insight into the meaning of the rule prior to using it to focus options.

Brainstorming Tool Lessons

Lesson 3—The Balloons and the Brainstormy Day. The purpose of this lesson is to introduce the brainstorming tool. Brainstorming is the generating tool most teachers are familiar with, and it is the most widely used generating tool. This lesson provides the basics of brainstorming, including following the four guidelines to generate many, varied, and unusual ideas for the imaginary situation of a balloon traveling to a magical place.

Lesson 4—The Squirrelly Brainstorm. The purpose of this lesson is to provide an additional opportunity to use the brainstorming tool. In this lesson, brainstorming is used to generate ideas for the problem of a squirrel who likes to take ripe peaches from the peach tree. This lesson provides the opportunity for the students to use a well-stated problem statement to generate ideas on a specific problem.

Going Beyond an Introduction to Brainstorming. The purpose of this short section is to provide the basic outline to follow anytime you want to generate using the brainstorming tool. Brainstorming can be used to generate many different kinds of options such as ideas, problems, or criteria. It can be used anytime there is a need to generate creative options, and it lends itself to the generation of a wide variety of different types of options. We include an example of steps to follow when using a well-stated, concise problem statement to generate ideas using brainstorming.

Braindrawing Tool Lessons

Lesson 5—The Amazing Braindrawing Machine. The purpose of this lesson is to introduce the braindrawing tool by generating ideas for new and unusual machines. Braindrawing is a generating tool that provides opportunities for many ideas by drawing on a worksheet and trading the sheets. This encourages students to get ideas for drawings from the other students' drawings.

Lesson 6—Drawing the Brainy Woodpecker. The purpose of this lesson is to provide an additional opportunity to use the braindrawing tool. In this lesson, braindrawing is used to generate ideas for the problem of a woodpecker disturbing the classroom by pecking on the window sill. This lesson provides the opportunity for the students to use a well-stated problem statement to generate ideas on a specific problem.

Going Beyond an Introduction to Braindrawing. The purpose of this short section is to provide the basic outline to follow anytime you want to generate using the braindrawing tool. Braindrawing can be used to generate many different kinds of options such as ideas, problems, or criteria. It can be used anytime there is a need to generate creative options, and it lends itself to the generation of a wide variety of different types of options. Braindrawing is a particularly good tool to generate many options by piggybacking off of other ideas, and it often provides a more comfortable generating environment for students who prefer drawing ideas rather than verbalizing ideas. We include an example of steps to follow when using a well-stated, concise problem statement to generate ideas using braindrawing.

Forced Relationships Tool Lessons

Lesson 7—Stamping Out Forced Relationships. The purpose of this lesson is to introduce the generating tool forced relationship. Stamps of different types of transportation are combined to come up with unique car ideas. Students stamp two modes of transportation on the worksheet and draw the resulting idea for a new type of transportation.

Lesson 8—Force a Stuffed Relationship. The purpose of this lesson is to provide an additional opportunity to use the forced relationship tool. Students can "force" stuffed animals together, drawing the resulting idea on Post-it® paper to share with the group. This provides a hands-on activity for students, which results in unique designs for stuffed animals.

Going Beyond an Introduction to Forced Relationships. The purpose of this short section is to provide the basic outline to follow anytime you want to generate using the forced relationship tool. Forced relationships can be used to generate many different kinds of options such as ideas, problems, or criteria. It can be used anytime there is a need to generate creative options, and it lends itself to generation of unique options. It is a good tool to use along with the brainstorming tool. We include an example of steps to follow when using a well-stated, concise problem statement to generate ideas using forced relationships.

SCAMPER Tool Lessons

Lesson 9—SCAMPER with LEGO® toys. The purpose of this lesson is to introduce the generating tool SCAMPER. SCAMPER stands for substitute, combine, adapt, modify, put to other uses, eliminate, and rearrange. Unique houses are developed by asking students SCAMPER questions to change a building they've made with LEGO® toys. This hands-on lesson allows students to manipulate the blocks to get ideas for different types of buildings.

Lesson 10—Invent a SCAMPER Chair. The purpose of this lesson is to provide an additional opportunity to use the SCAMPER tool for generating options. Ideas for changing a chair are drawn for each letter of SCAMPER on a worksheet. This provides a wide variety of different ideas for chair designs using each letter of SCAMPER.

Going Beyond an Introduction to SCAMPER. The purpose of this short section is to provide the basic outline to follow anytime you want to generate using the SCAMPER tool.

SCAMPER is a checklist of questions that can be used to generate many different kinds of options such as ideas, problems, or criteria. It can be used anytime there is a need to generate creative options, and it lends itself to generation of a wide variety of unique options. SCAMPER questions can be used independently, but they also can be used in conjunction with the brainstorming tool. We include an example of steps to follow when using a well-stated, concise problem statement to generate ideas using SCAMPER.

Hits Tool Lessons

Lesson 11—Hollywood Hits. The purpose of this lesson is to introduce the focusing tool called hits. A variety of popular movies are displayed, and students are asked to select their favorites using hits. Students place their hit dots on their favorites, and the most popular ones are discussed.

Lesson 12—Squirrel Away the Hits. The purpose of this lesson is to provide an additional opportunity to use the hits tools. Using the ideas generated in the Squirrelly Brainstorm lesson, students are asked to select the ideas they think will help solve the problem using hits.

Going Beyond an Introduction to Hits. The purpose of this short section is to provide the basic outline to follow anytime you want to focus using the hits tool. Hits can be used to focus many different kinds of options such as ideas, problems, or criteria. It can be used anytime there is a need to analyze, evaluate, and select creative options. Hits is best used to narrow down a large number of options. We include an example of steps to follow when evaluating and selecting ideas using hits.

Highlighting Tool Lessons

Lesson 13—Use Your Noodle to Highlight. The purpose of this lesson is to introduce the focusing tool called highlighting. Students select a variety of colored noodles and glue them on an ice cream cone worksheet, dividing them into three categories. This lesson provides a hands-on example of how objects or ideas can be selected and sorted into groups.

Lesson 14—Highlighting the Best of Everyone. This lesson provides additional opportunity to focus and group using highlighting. Students are grouped into a category of their choosing, such as hair length or color. This provides an opportunity for students to categorize and examine groupings.

Going Beyond an Introduction to Highlighting. The purpose of this short section is to provide the basic outline to follow anytime you want to focus using the highlighting tool. Highlighting can be used to focus many different kinds of options such as ideas, problems, or criteria. It can be used anytime there is a need to analyze, evaluate, and select creative options. Highlighting is used to compress a large number of ideas that lend themselves to grouping into categories. We include an example of steps to follow when evaluating and selecting ideas using highlighting.

Evaluation Matrix Tool Lessons

Lesson 15—Matrix Madness. The purpose of this lesson is to introduce the focusing tool called matrix. Students select their favorite pet stickers and rate the choices against criteria on a matrix worksheet. Both the pet choices and the smile, so-so, and frown face rating system provide an easy visual for students to examine. This visual lesson allows students to think about the good and bad points of each pet.

Lesson 16—Matrix by the Sea. This lesson provides an additional opportunity to use the matrix tool. Students select their favorite sea shells and rate them against criteria.

Going Beyond an Introduction to Matrix. The purpose of this short section is to provide the basic outline to follow anytime you want to focus using the matrix tool. The matrix can be used to focus many different kinds of options such as ideas, problems, or solutions. It can be used anytime there is a need to analyze, evaluate, and develop creative options. The matrix is used to evaluate a number of options against criteria. The options can then be analyzed and improved for implementation. We include an example of steps to follow when evaluating and selecting ideas using the matrix.

ALoU Tool Lessons

Lesson 17—The Game of ALoU. The purpose of this lesson is to introduce the focusing tool ALoU. Students play a game and then use the ALoU tool to positively evaluate the game-playing experience. This provides a systematic way to evaluate the game, starting with the advantages, then listing limitations in the form of a question, examining uniqueness, and finally selecting some of the limitations and generating ideas to improve the game.

Lesson 18—Designing a Stuffed Animal ALoU. The purpose of this lesson is to provide an additional opportunity to use the ALoU. The drawings from the Force a Stuffed Relationship lessons are evaluated and improved by examining the advantages, limitations, and uniqueness, and then overcoming a limitation.

Going Beyond an Introduction to ALoU. The purpose of this short section is to provide the basic outline to follow anytime you want to focus using the ALoU tool. The ALoU can be used to focus many different kinds of options such as ideas, problems, or criteria. It can be used anytime there is a need to positively analyze, evaluate, and develop creative options. The ALoU is used to evaluate one, two, or three options and improve the options by overcoming the key limitations. We include an example of steps to follow when evaluating and selecting ideas using the ALoU.

Materials for CPS Tools

The materials listed in the Material Kit should be kept on hand anytime you work with *Big Tools for Young Thinkers*. In addition to gathering a Material Kit, we suggest that you make posters to outline the generating and focusing rules and the generating and focusing tools in words and pictures. The materials needed are listed below.

Chart paper	Pencils
Crayons	Post-its®
Drawing Paper	Small Toys
Markers	Stickers and Dots
Masking Tape	

Visuals are an important way to aid in students' understanding of these concepts. The generating tools chart should be made with green construction paper to represent generating, and the focusing tool charts should be made with red construction paper to represent focusing (see diagram below). In addition, it is helpful to include an illustration or diagram to represent the tool (i.e., braindrawing form next to braindrawing).

Generating Tools	Focusing Tools
Brainstorming	Hits
Braindrawing	Highlighting
SCAMPER	ALoU
Forced Relationships	Matrix

The generating rules chart should be made with green construction paper to represent generating, and the focusing rules chart should be made with red construction paper to represent focusing (see diagram below). A picture representing each rule is helpful (see Generating and Focusing Rules Lessons for suggestions).

Generating Rules	Focusing Rules
Don't Judge	Be Positive
Lots of Ideas	Look at New Items
Wild & Crazy	Use Your Head
Piggyback	Look Where You're Going

Free Thinking and Happy Judgment

Deferring judgment ("Don't judge!" in kid terms) is the most important basic principle that underlies all generating strategies and efforts. So, generating or diverging can be a gas if you put the gas pedal to the metal and go to green light thinking. Whenever you are generating creative ideas, you should deliberately refrain from judging (no ifs, ands, or buts about it!). Research and practice, since the outlining of deferred judgment by Osborn (1953) strongly supports this as a key factor in effective generating.

The flip side of deferring judgment is the need to use affirmative judgment, or "being positive" in kid terms. So, focusing or converging switches on the brake to stop and do some red light thinking. It is important to take a constructive, not destructive approach to evaluation. Critical thinking does not mean negative thinking. Don't attack ideas; rather, select what fits for you and focus on the ideas you want to use, not the ones you dislike.

The four rules to follow when generating include: Don't Judge, Lots of Ideas, Wild & Crazy, and Piggyback. The four rules to follow when focusing include: Be Positive, Look at New Items, Use Your Head, and Look Where You're Going. The rules are described in the first two lessons in this book and on page 6, in the Generating and Focusing Rules.

A Place for Creativity

One way to avoid problems when generating ideas is to solve potential problems before they happen. For example, suppose you are brainstorming (and therefore deferring judgment), and a child throws out an idea describing a classmate as stupid. What do you do? If you immediately explain that we don't say nasty things about each other, you've stopped deferring judgment. Of course, what the child said was inappropriate, and as a teacher you don't tolerate this type of behavior. Remember, however, that in order to follow the principle of deferring judgment (which is essential!), you don't want to judge at *all* during a session. Therefore, it's important to set up the expectations for how we treat each other before you begin using the tools. Set up your expectations for how we treat others before you start generating by examining aspects of a creative climate so that you avoid situations like name calling. Here's a "snapshot" of some of the pieces of a creative climate (see Ekvall, 1991) that can help you build a creative climate in your classroom:

1. Listen to all ideas.
2. Feel free to be different.
3. Allow for freedom of choice.
4. Stretch your brain.
5. It's OK to disagree.
6. It's not OK to fight or hurt other's feelings.
7. Go ahead and try new things.
8. Take time to think.
9. Make it fun.

What A Team!

Most of the tools described in this book, particularly the generating tool, are designed for group application. Therefore, it is important to stress the concept of a team working together. Students should be encouraged to work as a team and avoid the words "mine" or "my idea." Explain that each idea generated is a valuable part of the team effort, and it doesn't matter who said the idea or which ideas are selected. This is particularly important to emphasize when you ask students to share some ideas they like after a generating session.

A Bit of a Problem

Once you've tried the lessons in this book, you're ready to move on to using the tools with a variety of problems or situations. The *Going Beyond an Introduction to Brainstorming* outlined in this book, for example, explains how to use brainstorming with any problem or issue. Problems, however are not created equal! Some problems are more carefree and fun. Others are deeper, more personal concerns that will involve much more time and effort on the part of the group. Dewey said "a well-stated problem is half solved." The appropriate selection of the kinds of problems to work on in a generating session and their proper wording is essential for a successful learning experience for students. We suggest that a well-stated, concise problem statement starting with an invitational stem such as "How to … ?" will be a good beginning. Included in Appendix B are references, such as *Creative Problem Solving: An Introduction* and *Creative Approaches to Problem Solving,* for selecting issues for creative problem solving and formulating problem statements. For examples of problems, you can use *Practice Problems for Creative Problem Solving* or *Be a Problem Solver.*

How to Capture Ideas?

After applying principles of deferring judgement and affirmative judgment, the most difficult task a teacher has is figuring out how to write down all the ideas his or her fluent thinkers are eagerly ready to share during a generating session. Here are a few tips. The easiest way to record ideas is to work with a small group of 7 to 10 students. If you must work with larger size groups or whole classrooms, you can still manage to record all the ideas. We suggest that you write as quickly as you can, capturing the child's ideas in short phrases. Another way to do this is to give all your students Post-its® and have them write or draw one idea per note, say it, and then hand it to you to put on the chart. Another method is to have older students work with small groups to record their ideas. Make sure your older students are trained in the concept of deferring judgment and are therefore willing to write down all the ideas without reacting to them in any way.

Lesson 1

GENERATING RULES

Purpose: To understand the rules of generating options.

Key Point: The students learn the four rules for generating options by developing illustrations for them.

Materials & Preparation:

Generating rules
Strips of green paper
Drawing paper
Write one rule on each strip of green paper.

Warm Up: Show students the generating rules. Explain that whenever we want to do some green light thinking or come up with ideas, we'll follow the generating rules. Explain each rule to the class.

Don't judge means that when we come up with ideas, we don't worry about whether they are good or bad. It's important to just say what comes to your head and not worry if it's a good idea. Also, we don't say anything at all about other people's ideas.

Lots of ideas means we want to come up with at least 30 ideas or many more than that, depending on what we are working on.

Wild & Crazy means we can come up with ideas that are silly, far out, and strange.

Piggyback means we can think of ideas off another person's ideas. It's OK to copy a person's idea and change it a bit.

Digging Deeper:

1. Give small groups of students one rule written on green paper and review the meaning of the rule.

2. In small groups, discuss all the drawings you might make to go with the rule.

3. Ask each small group to individually draw a picture explaining their rule.

Extension:

1. Display pictures of each rule.

2. Have each group share their pictures and explain the rule to the class.

3. Debrief the learning: What did we do in this lesson? What are the four rules? What is the smallest amount of ideas we want? Could we do more than that? Why? Why is it important not to judge? What does it mean to be wild and crazy? How do you piggyback? When do we use these rules?

Enhancements:

Understanding the generating rules is an essential prerequisite for using any of the generating tools. Additional time spent with students helping them understand the rules is time well-spent. Some activities might include looking over a list of brainstormed ideas and pointing out the results of each rule. For example, point out ideas that came from piggybacking, ones that are wild, and look at the number of ideas generated. Talk to students about how well they deferred judgment. You might ask them if there were any ideas they thought of that they did not share and why. Discuss whether anyone judged by making comments (negative or positive) during the generating. Another activity might center around comparing generating and judging each idea immediately after presented versus waiting until they were all generated to evaluate.

Lesson 2
FOCUSING RULES

Purpose: To understand the rules for focusing options.

Key Point: The students learn the four rules for focusing options by developing illustrations for them.

Materials & Preparation: Focusing rules
Strips of red paper
Drawing paper
Write one rule on each strip of red paper.

Warm Up: Show students the focusing rules. Explain that whenever we want to do some red light thinking or pick ideas, we follow the focusing rules. Explain each rule to the class.

Be Positive means we pick ideas by saying the ones we like, not complaining or crossing out ones we dislike.

Look at New Items means don't forget about an idea that might be a bit weird. Think about whether it might be good, also.

Use Your Head means plan out the tools you'll use and the choices that are best for you.

Look Where You're Going means know what your goal is and keep your eyes on that target.

Digging Deeper:
1. Give small groups of students one rule written on red construction paper and review the meaning of the rule.

2. In small groups, discuss all the drawings you might make to go with the rule.

3. Ask each small group to individually draw a picture explaining their rule.

Extension:
1. Display pictures of each rule.

2. Have each group share their pictures and explain them to the class.

3. Debrief the learning: What did we do in this lesson? What are the four rules? Why is it important to be positive? What does it mean to "look at the new"? How do you use the tools? When do we use these rules?

Enhancements:
Understanding the focusing rules is an essential prerequisite for using any of the focusing tools. Additional time spent with students helping them understand the rules is time well-spent. For example, find some examples of some far out ideas that ended up working and use those examples to explain the importance of considering the ideas that are far out or very new. Examine the difference between affirmative judgement (positive judgement) and negative judgement (such as pointing out all of the dumb ideas). Examine the importance of setting goals as a way to achieve outcomes.

Lesson 3

THE BALLOONS AND THE BRAINSTORMY DAY

Purpose: To generate many, varied, and unusual ideas using brainstorming.

Key Point: Introduce brainstorming as a generating tool. Generate a whole bunch of ideas for the magical fun the balloons had on the Brainstormy Day using the brainstorming tool.

Materials & Preparation: Balloons of various shapes and sizes
Fan

Warm Up:

1. Review generating rules.

2. Display balloons.

3. Make up a story about lonely balloons that want to have some fun. Explain how a strange Brainstormy wind blew the balloon to a magically fun place. Use a fan to blow the balloons to a magical place.

Digging Deeper:

1. Ask students to tell all about the magical fun the balloons had on the Brainstormy day. Remind them to follow the generating rules while they brainstorm about all the magically fun places the lonely balloons might go.

2. Write all the ideas the students have under the heading "The Balloons and the Brainstormy Day."

3. Encourage students to think of as many ideas as fast as they can and to throw in some wild and crazy ones, too.

Extension:

1. Ask students to share their favorite ideas. (Reread the list if necessary.)

2. Debrief the learning: What did you notice about brain-

storming? What did you like about brainstorming? How did we do generating wild and crazy ideas? Can you give an example? How did we do with piggybacking? Not judging? Getting lots of ideas? (Have students give examples for each generating rule.) How does brainstorming help us get lots of ideas?

Enhancements:

1. Brainstorming can also be done with a small group of students.

2. Brainstorming is an extremely versatile generating tool that can provide the opportunity to strengthen comprehension of the generating rules while learning the tool. While generating using the brainstorming tool, remind students of the rules, one at a time, throughout the lesson. Keep track of which ideas were generated while a rule was reinforced. After the session, go back and look at the types of ideas generated (or, in the case of the "lots of ideas rule," look at the volume of ideas in a time period) while a particular rule was reinforced.

Lesson 4
THE SQUIRRELLY BRAINSTORM

Purpose: To generate many, varied, and unusual ideas using brainstorming.

Key Point: Use brainstorming to generate ideas to solve the squirrel problem.

Materials & Preparation: A picture of a squirrel

Warm Up:
1. Review generating rules.

2. Explain that you're tired of going into the backyard to pick a ripe peach only to find that the squirrel stole it.

3. Write the problem statement, "How to stop the squirrel from taking my peaches?" on the top of the chart paper and explain that you don't want to hurt the squirrel. You need their help in coming up with creative ideas.

Digging Deeper:
1. Have students brainstorm ideas for the problem statement, "How to stop the squirrel from taking my peaches?" Strive for at least 35 ideas.

2. Throughout brainstorming, remind students of the problem statement and the generating rules.

Extension:
1. Students share some of their favorite ideas.

2. Debrief the learning: What did you notice? How did we do getting ideas? What were some examples of piggybacking, wild and crazy, not judging? Why do we brainstorm ideas for a problem? How can this help with my squirrel problem?

3. Save the ideas generated to be used in the hits lesson.

Enhancements: Instead of the teacher writing the ideas, the students can draw or write their idea on a Post-it®, say it (so everyone can hear it), and then hand it to the teacher to be placed on the chart paper for all to see.

GOING BEYOND AN INTRODUCTION TO BRAINSTORMING

You can use brainstorming to generate creative options (i.e., ideas, problem statements, or criteria to evaluate options). For example, here are some steps to follow when you generate ideas:

1. List on chart paper a topic or problem that needs creative ideas. Phrase problem statements starting with "How to … ?" to invite lots of ideas.

2. Review generating rules.

3. Generate at least 35 ideas for the topic or problem statement. List on the chart.

4. Remind students of the rules as they generate.

Lesson 5

THE AMAZING BRAINDRAWING MACHINE

Purpose: To generate many, varied, and unusual machines using braindrawing.

Key Point: Introduce braindrawing as a generating tool. Piggyback off of other machine ideas to build many different machines using braindrawing.

Materials & Preparation: Braindrawing Worksheet
Various machines or machine parts (TV, computer, VCR, video games, phone, cables, calculator) or pictures of various machines.
Paste pictures of machines on poster board.

Warm Up:
1. Let students touch and discuss the various machines. List additional machines not shown.

2. Explain that we're going to generate the most amazing machines. Review generating rules.

3. Give out one braindrawing form for each student. Explain that this is not their sheet, they should not put their name on it, and that they will be giving it away soon.

Digging Deeper:
1. Have students draw three ideas across the top row for the most amazing machine they've ever seen. Tell students this super machine can be made of anything and do anything you want. All you have to do is use your imagination.

2. Have students in pairs share the three ideas for amazing machines.

3. Switch braindrawing worksheets with a partner.

4. Encourage students to draw three more ideas for an Amazing Machine below their partners' three. Encourage students to piggyback off of the partners' ideas; but, since you want to continue to follow the generating rules, do not limit to piggybacking only.

Extension:

1. Display finished forms for the group to see. Ask students to point to and explain an idea for an Amazing Machine they like. (Reinforce that they should not say, "my idea"; rather they should say, "I like this idea.")

2. Ask students to point out examples of piggybacking.

3. Debrief the learning: What did we do? How does piggybacking help us come up with ideas? What did you like about braindrawing? How does braindrawing work? What are the steps to fill in the braindrawing form? How did braindrawing help us come up with ideas? Review each rule by asking students, "What does this rule mean?"

Enhancements:

The braindrawing form can be made simpler by only having two rows of two blocks (four rectangles total) or more challenging by having four rows of four blocks (12 rectangles total). The more challenging version allows students to create more machines in each turn and to switch sheets twice instead of once.

Lesson 6
DRAWING THE BRAINY WOODPECKER

Purpose:	To generate many, varied, and unusual options using braindrawing.
Key Point:	Use the braindrawing tool to solve the problem of a noisy woodpecker pecking at my window sill early in the morning.
Materials & Preparation:	Braindrawing Worksheet Optional: Place a picture of a woodpecker outside the classroom window.
Warm Up:	1. Review generating rules. 2. Explain that we're going to work on the problem of the brainy woodpecker who likes to peck on the window sill early in the morning. 3. Write the problem statement, "How to stop the woodpecker from pecking on the windowsill?" on the top of the braindrawing form. Explain that you'll need their help in coming up with ideas. 4. Remind students that we work as a team whenever we generate ideas, and the sheet you're about to give them is not their sheet, but belongs to the team. Show students the braindrawing sheet and explain that they should not write their name on it because they will be trading it shortly.
Digging Deeper:	1. Across the top of the braindrawing form, have students draw three ideas for stopping the woodpecker. 2. Students share the three ideas with a partner and then switch forms. 3. Draw three more ideas across the second row of the paper. Ask students to look at the top row of ideas that their part-

ner drew and try to come up with ideas piggybacking off of those and/or come up with new ideas, too.

4. Share drawings, switch papers with the same partner, and draw ideas across the last row.

Extension:

1. Display finished forms for the group to see. Ask students to point out ideas they liked and share them.

2. Debrief the learning: What did we do? How does piggybacking help us come up with ideas? What did you like about braindrawing? How does braindrawing work? What are the steps to fill in the form? What do the generating rules mean? How did brainwriting help us solve the problem?

Enhancements:

More advanced students can also write a caption, title, or sentence for each drawing or simply use words instead of pictures to represent the ideas.

BRAINDRAWING

GOING BEYOND AN INTRODUCTION TO BRAINDRAWING

You can use braindrawing to generate creative options (i.e. ideas, problem statements, or criteria to evaluate options). For example, here are some steps to follow when you generate ideas:

1. List on the top of a braindrawing form a topic or problem statement that needs creative ideas. Start problem statements with "How to … ?" to invite ideas.

2. Review generating rules and remind students that you work as a team to braindraw.

3. Have students draw three ideas for the problem across the top of the paper.

4. In pairs, have students share ideas and switch papers.

5. Students draw three more ideas, possibly piggybacking off the ideas drawn in the row above.

6. Repeat the sharing and trading until sheet is complete.

Lesson 7

STAMPING OUT FORCED RELATIONSHIPS

Purpose: To generate many, varied, and unusual ideas using forced relationships.

Key Point: Introduce a generating tool called forced relationships. Force two different modes of transportation stamps together to come up with a new idea for a mode of transportation.

Materials & Preparation: Various modes of transportation stamps or stickers (Small magazine pictures or drawings of different modes of transportation can be used if stamps or stickers are unavailable.)
Stamp Pads
Forced Relationships Equation Worksheet

Warm Up:
1. Review generating rules and explain that we're going to do forced relationships, a tool for generating ideas or green light thinking.

2. On a sample worksheet, show students how to complete the worksheet by stamping two different modes of transportation such as car and bike on each side of the plus sign and drawing a new design you've made up after the equal sign.

3. Do several examples together and share the forced relationships. Remind students to draw whatever comes to mind from forcing the two stamps together.

Digging Deeper:
1. Give materials to each student and allow them to complete the Forced Relationship Equation Worksheet individually.

2. Periodically switch the stamps at each table to provide variety.

Extension:
1. Pair students to share the equations.

2. Share some of the favorite equations in a large group.

3. Debrief the learning: What did you notice? What did you like about this lesson? What did you do with the stamps? How did you think of the designs you drew? What does it mean to make forced relationships? What do we do when we generate or do green light thinking? How do the generating rules help us come up with ideas for new design? How does forced relationships help us come up with ideas?

Enhancements:

1. Use stickers instead of stamps on the worksheet.

2. When working on a unit of study such as community helpers, use stamps or stickers that correspond to the unit.

Lesson 8

FORCE A STUFFED RELATIONSHIP

Purpose:

To generate many, varied and unusual ideas using forced relationships.

Key Point:

Use the forced relationship tool to design a new stuffed animal by forcing a relationship between two different stuffed animals.

Materials & Preparation:

Many, varied, and unusual stuffed animals

Warm Up:

1. Review generating rules.

2. Display lots of stuffed animals.

3. Discuss how designers can get an idea for a new stuffed animal by forcing two different animals together to make up a new one.

Digging Deeper:

1. Have students take two animals, put them together in their mind, and draw an idea for a new stuffed animal on a Post-it®.

2. Share ideas and display on chart paper.

3. Continue to generate new designs by forcing two stuffed animals together and drawing the new idea on a Post-it® (Save ideas for Designing a Stuffed Animal ALoU lesson.)

Extension:

1. Review the new designs listed on chart paper. Share the ones the students like in pairs and then in a large group. Ask students to share examples and explain which objects they forced together.

2. Debrief the learning: What do you notice about the ideas? How did we use the objects to get ideas? How does forcing relationships help us get ideas?

Enhancements:

1. Use stuffed animals the students can hold and force together. Draw the resulting animals on paper.

2. Force together various other types of objects by placing them in front of students during a session so they can freely pick them up and make connections.

3. Baggies with different smells or objects that make noise can also be used.

FORCED RELATIONSHIP EQUATION

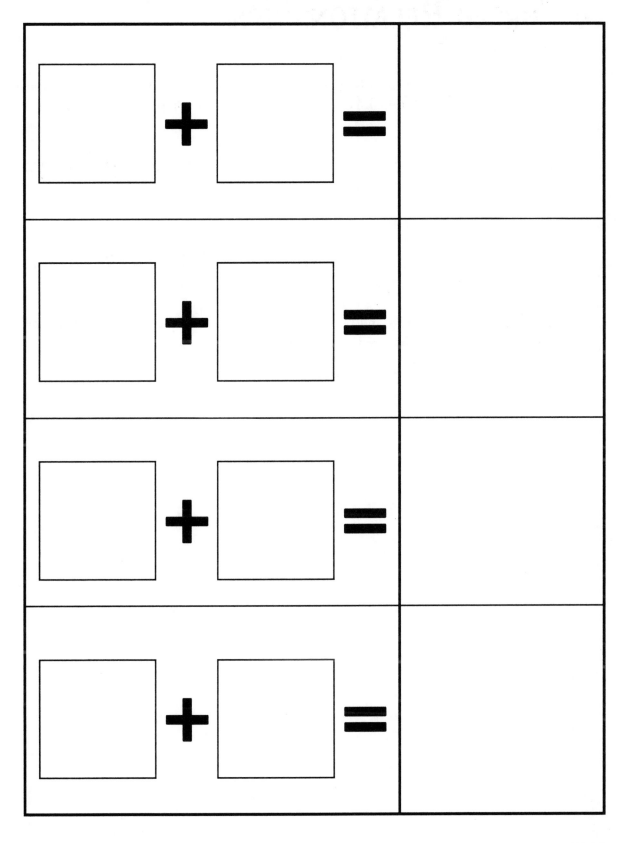

GOING BEYOND AN INTRODUCTION TO FORCED RELATIONSHIPS

You can use Forced Relationships to generate creative options (i.e. ideas, problem statements, or criteria to evaluate options). For example, here are some steps to follow when you generate ideas:

1. Choose a problem or topic which needs creative ideas. Phrase the problem starting with "How to … ?" to invite ideas.

2. Begin by generating at least 10–15 ideas on large chart paper.

3. Hold up an object or picture and ask students to describe it. Then ask "What ideas can you get from this to solve the problem?"

4. Continue to generate ideas and use several other objects or pictures throughout the session to stimulate the production of many ideas.

Lesson 9

SCAMPER WITH LEGO® TOYS

Purpose:	To generate many, varied, and unusual ideas using SCAMPER.
Key Point:	Introduce a generating tool called SCAMPER. Build different houses by substituting, combining, adapting, modifying, putting to other uses, eliminating, and rearranging the LEGO® toys.
Materials & Preparation:	LEGO® toys Write the word SCAMPER vertically on chart paper. Next to each letter write the word it stands for (i.e., S = Substitute).

Warm Up:

1. Review generating rules.

2. Introduce the SCAMPER words in the chart and tell students that we're going to think of all kinds of strange and unusual houses to build using the SCAMPER words.

Digging Deeper:

1. Ask students to build houses with LEGO® toys.

2. Ask students to substitute by taking a piece of the house off and put some other pieces on in its place.

3. Have volunteers share their examples of substituting.

4. Repeat by asking questions for each letter of SCAMPER:

Substitute:	Take a piece of the house off and put some other pieces on in its place.
Combine:	Take two structures you built and put them together.
Adapt:	Change some part of your house.

Modify:	Look over your building and make something smaller, or make something bigger.
Put to other Uses:	How else could you use your house? Change it so that you can use it for something other than just a house.
Eliminate:	Get rid of something.
Rearrange:	Change your building around, mix it up.

Extension:

1. Share the final buildings in a large group and explain how they changed. Have students explain changes they made from the SCAMPER questions.

2. Debrief the learning: What do you notice about the buildings? What is the same? What is different about them? What do you like about them? What did we do with the SCAMPER words? What did you like about SCAMPER? How does SCAMPER help you get ideas for new toy houses? How did the generating rules help you get ideas?

Enhancements:

Instead of using LEGO® toys, use the SCAMPER worksheet or create your own worksheet by dividing a paper in eight. Have students draw a house in the first square. Put one letter of SCAMPER in each other squares leaving room for an additional drawing in the square. Guide students through the SCAMPER questions, having them draw their idea for changes in each square.

Lesson 10

INVENT A SCAMPER CHAIR

Purpose: To generate many, varied, and unusual ideas using SCAMPER.

Key Point: Use the SCAMPER tool to think like an inventor to change a chair.

Materials & Preparation: SCAMPER Worksheet
Examples of different types of chairs
Paste chair example to poster board

Warm Up:
1. Review generating rules.

2. Discuss how inventors often take ordinary objects and change them to come up with new inventions.

3. Show various examples of different types of chairs.

Digging Deeper:
1. Give students a SCAMPER worksheet and ask them to draw a chair in the first square.

2. Describe each letter of SCAMPER on the sheet and explain that they are going to generate ideas for different chairs using the words.

3. Have students draw an idea in the substitute box by taking something off the chair and putting something else in its place.

4. Repeat with the rest of the letters of SCAMPER:

  Combine: Combine your chair with a different type of chair and draw what it looks like.

  Adapt: Change something on the chair to make it different.

Modify:	What can you make smaller or bigger to make the chair different?
Put to Other Uses:	What else could you use a chair for besides sitting? Change it so it can be used for something else.
Eliminate:	What can you get rid of on the chair to make it better?
Rearrange:	What can you mix up or move around on the chair to make it different?

Extension:

1. Review the generated list. Share the ones the students like in pairs, and then in a large group.

2. Debrief the learning: What do you notice about the ideas? How did we solve this problem? What do the letters in SCAMPER mean? Give an example of an idea you thought of for *Substitute*? *Combine*? and so forth. How did we use SCAMPER? How does SCAMPER help solve problems?

Enhancements:

1. Parts of SCAMPER or any other idea-spurring checklist can be used independently of the other letters as idea-spurring questions whenever generating ideas.

2. Next to each letter on the SCAMPER chart, add an example of an object (such as a chair) that has been changed using this method.

	SUBSTITUTE	COMBINE	ADAPT
IDEA			
MODIFY	PUT TO OTHER USES	ELIMINATE	REARRANGE

GOING BEYOND AN INTRODUCTION TO SCAMPER

You can use SCAMPER to generate creative options (i.e., ideas, problem statements, or criteria to evaluate options). For example, here are some steps to follow when you generate ideas:

1. List on chart paper a topic or problem statement that needs creative ideas. Begin problems with "How to … ?" to invite ideas.

2. Review generating rules.

3. Begin by generating at least 10–15 ideas on large chart paper.

4. Ask students SCAMPER questions to spur more ideas throughout the generating session. An example of a key word for each include:

Substitute:	What can you take off and put back in its place to solve the problem?
Combine:	What two things can you put together to help solve this problem?
Adapt:	Change something on the chair to make it different. How can you change something to solve this problem?
Modify:	What can you make smaller or bigger to solve this problem?
Put to Other Uses:	What can you use in a different way to solve the problem?
Eliminate:	What can you get rid of to solve the problem?
Rearrange:	What can you mix up or move around to solve this problem?

Lesson 11

HOLLYWOOD HITS

Purpose: To focus or narrow down a large number of options using hits.

Key Point: Introduce a focusing tool called hits. From a large list of movies, select some movies that students really like.

Materials & Preparation: Popular kid movie posters or video box covers
Round stickers or dots
Large Post-it® paper
Place large Post-it® paper under each movie. Write the name of the movie on the Post-it®.

Warm Up:
1. Review focusing rules.

2. Have students discuss the different movies.

Digging Deeper:
1. Give each student five to seven dots and ask them to select their favorite movies. (A large piece of Post-it® paper under each poster or box can be used to place the dots called "hits.") Hits are ideas that "sparkle" or stand out as ones that might help. Tell students, "It is okay to put your dot on any of the choices whether it already has many dots or whether it doesn't have any at all."

Extension:
1. On chart paper, display the dots for each movie and discuss which were the most popular. Have students share what they like about some of the chosen movies.

2. Discuss how we were able to quickly focus on a fewer number of movies using hits.

3. Debrief the learning: What did we do? How were we able to narrow down such a large number of movies so fast? What are the hits? How do hits help us make choices?

Enhancements:

1. After discussing the hits, have the students put the movies in order of hits from largest to smallest number.

2. Use many objects the students can hold, such as small character toys or matchbox cars instead of movies.

Lesson 12

SQUIRREL AWAY THE HITS

Purpose:

To focus a large number of ideas down to a smaller number using hits.

Key Point:

Use the hits tool to focus and narrow down the ideas to solve the problem of the noisy squirrel.

Materials & Preparation:

Ideas generated from the lesson The Squirrelly Brainstorm
Dot stickers

Warm Up:

1. Review focusing rules.

2. Review the ideas generated to solve the problem, "How to stop the squirrel from stealing the peaches?"

Digging Deeper:

1. Give each student several dots.

2. Ask the students to dot the ideas that are "hits." Remind students not to forget some that they like, even if the ideas are different or weird.

Extension:

1. Review the hit list and discuss why they think the chosen hits are good choices.

2. Debrief the learning: What do you notice about the ideas chosen? Did you pick some that were a little different? How did you choose from so many ideas? How are hits like voting? How are they different than voting?

Enhancements:

1. Hits can be rewritten on separate paper or on individual Post-its® once selected.

2. Chart the hits on a bar graph by placing large Post-it® paper with hits under each bar in the graph and coloring the bar for each.

GOING BEYOND AN INTRODUCTION TO HITS

You can use hits to narrow down a large number of options (i.e., ideas, problem statements, or criteria to evaluation options). For example, here are some steps to follow when you select ideas using hits:

1. Review focusing rules.

2. Discuss and list the key data and list of ideas generated on chart paper.

3. Give the client (or whole class if it's a group problem) a pack of dots.

4. Ask the client to dot the ideas that are "hits." Hits are ideas that "sparkle" or stand out as ones that might help. Remind the client not to forget to look closely at the very novel ideas, as well.

5. Review the hit list. Have the client share the chosen ideas and talk about why they were chosen.

Lesson 13

USE YOUR NOODLE TO HIGHLIGHT

Purpose:

To focus on a select number of options and narrow down the choices by grouping them using highlighting.

Key Point:

Introduce a focusing tool called highlighting. Select the noodles you like the best (hits), sort them into groupings (relates), and make a name or title for each related group (hot spots).

Materials & Preparation:

Many, varied, noodles (various shapes, sizes, and colors are helpful) Highlighting Ice Cream Cone Worksheet

Warm Up:

1. Look over the various kinds of noodles and share what you see.

2. Explain how, very often, a cook has to choose the ones he or she likes best to make a recipe.

3. Allow students to take a whole bunch of noodles that they really like. Explain that these are their "hits" or favorite ones.

Digging Deeper:

1. Ask students to sort the noodles into like groups. Give examples if necessary.

2. Have students think about how they grouped them, share their thinking with a partner, and then share as a large group.

3. Have them name two or three groups and glue them on the ice cream cone worksheet.

Extension:

1. Share worksheets.

2. Debrief the learning: What did we do? What did you notice? What is a hit? How did you group these? What did you name it? Did anyone have a similar group? Did anyone

have something different? How many groups did you have? What did you like about highlighting? How did highlighting or grouping these help us to pick two (or three) to put on our ice cream cone sheet?

Enhancements:

1. Use any objects that can be easily grouped, such as marbles, seashells, buttons, or rocks.

2. Do groupings together as a class or in groups of three or four, if students have a difficult time with categorizing.

Lesson 14

HIGHLIGHTING THE BEST OF EVERYONE

Purpose:
To narrow options by compressing a large number of options using hits.

Key Point:
Use the highlighting tool to focus and group students into categories.

Materials & Preparation:
Poster board

Warm Up:
1. Review focusing rules.

2. Discuss how people in your class are different from each other (i.e., hair length or color).

Digging Deeper:
1. Select one way people in your class are different.

2. Have students discuss the groups that would be formed and move into groups to show the differences.

3. Ask each group to name themselves and hold up a sign to show the category (i.e., brown hair).

4. Explain how highlighting takes a big group and forms them into smaller groupings.

Extension:
1. Discuss how many different groups were formed.

2. Debrief the learning: What did we do? How did we narrow down to a few groups of people using highlighting?

Enhancements:
When working on a unit of study such as textures, use items that correspond to that unit to categorize using highlighting.

HIGHLIGHTING ICE CREAM CONE

GOING BEYOND AN INTRODUCTION TO HIGHLIGHTING

You can use highlighting to narrow down a large number of options (i.e., ideas, problem statements) that tend to relate to each other. For example, here are some steps to follow when you select ideas using highlighting:

1. Review focusing rules.

2. Select the hits.

3. Examine the hits and group ideas that relate to each other.

4. Name the groups.

Lesson 15

MATRIX MADNESS

| Purpose: | To focus or narrow to one or several choices by weighing the choices against criteria on a matrix. |

Purpose: To focus or narrow to one or several choices by weighing the choices against criteria on a matrix.

Key Point: Introduce a focusing tool called matrix. Rate several or many choices of pets against criteria in order to make a decision.

Materials & Preparation: Five or six different pet stickers per student
Matrix Worksheet
Cut out a class set of two-inch red, green, and yellow squares.
Draw a happy face on the green, so-so face on the yellow, and frown face on the red squares.
Draw a large sample matrix on chart paper.

Warm Up:
1. Review focusing rules.

2. Show students the four different pet stickers.

3. Discuss what makes a good pet. Brainstorm on chart paper all of the things a pet needs to be in order to be a good pet. (Criteria for a good pet might be clean, inexpensive, fun, easy to care for.) State them starting with "It must … " Select two to three criteria for what a pet must be.

Digging Deeper:
1. On a large sample matrix, fill in the two to three criteria choices across the top and the pet choices down the side. Give students matrix and pet stickers. Have them place the criteria and the pet stickers in the same order as the sample.

2. Give students three vote cards: green smile for great, yellow so-so face for maybe, and red frown face for no.

3. Using the large matrix, ask students, "If you make this choice (first pet on chart) will it be (first criterion listed)?" Ask students to show the card that tells how they feel. Survey the group and draw either a smile face, a so-so face, or a frown face according to how the majority of the class responded.

4. Have the students copy the face from the large sample matrix to their individual matrix. Remind them that they are drawing the same face as the large matrix (the face the majority of the class voted for), and it may be different from what they chose.

5. Repeat with choice 2, 3, and 4 against the first criterion. Then, go back to choices in order against the second and third criteria.

Extension:

1. Discuss the results of the matrix. Ask the students which pet choices look good to the class according to the criteria? Why? Which do not do as well against the criteria?

2. Explain that the winner is not necessarily the one with all the smiles. If we really like a lizard because we think it will be fun, but it's rated low on "easy to care for," we could brainstorm "How to take care of it?" and select some of the ideas that would make it easier to care for.

3. Debrief the learning: What did we do? What did you notice about the matrix? What did you like about the matrix? What criteria did we use? How do criteria help us make a decision? How does a matrix help us look at choices for pets?

Enhancements:

1. Use other stickers or stamps in place of the pet stickers.

2. Use the choices represented in a unit of study, such as dinosaurs or types of plants.

Lesson 16

MATRIX BY THE SEA

Purpose: To focus on evaluation, comparison, and development of a number of options using the matrix.

Key Point: Use the matrix tool to evaluate and select different sea shells against criteria.

Materials & Preparation: Many, varied, and unusual sea shells
Matrix Worksheet
Draw a large sample matrix on chart paper

Warm Up:

1. Review focusing rules.

2. Distribute many shells and let students look them over and talk about them.

3. Ask students what kind of shells they like. List what makes a shell a good one (i.e., whole not broken, lots of ridges, different colors on it, big, swirl, flat, symmetrical).

4. Select some reasons that are most important to the students (these criteria should be explicit, not "nice" or "pretty").

Digging Deeper:

1. On a large sample matrix, place three or four of your favorite shells vertically and two criteria horizontally across the top.

2. Complete the sample matrix as an example by asking, "If I pick shell 1, will it be (first criterion)?" Place a smile, so-so, or frown face in that box. Continue to rate each shell against the first criterion. Then rate the same shells against the second criterion. Talk to students about the result of your matrix and review how to do a matrix.

3. Let students pick three or four of their favorite shells and two criteria.

4. Students complete the matrix individually.

Extension:

1. Discuss results of the matrices.

2. Debrief the learning: What did we do? How did you decide which shells were the best? What are criteria? What criteria did you pick? Why? How did you know which shells were the best ones on the matrix?

Enhancements:

1. Once the students have practiced using the matrix, they might each rate the choices against the criteria separately, rather than filling it in as a whole group. More advanced students might be able to make the selection of the most important criteria independently.

2. For younger students, you could have the choices and criteria on the matrix before handing it out, or you could just do one large matrix as a group. Vote cards can then be used that allow each student to voice his or her choice.

3. You can vary the number of choices and the number of criteria depending on the ability of the students and the use of the matrix.

Yes

Maybe

No

Matrix

Criteria →

Ideas ↓

GOING BEYOND AN INTRODUCTION TO MATRIX

You can use the matrix to evaluate a number of ideas or possible solutions against criteria. Here are some steps to follow when you evaluate ideas against criteria:

1. Review focusing rules.

2. Discuss ideas selected.

3. List on chart paper what makes it a good idea (criteria). Ask students: "What does the idea have to be?" "What do you want the idea to be in order to do it or use it?" Select the most important criteria using hits.

4. Place chosen ideas (vertically) and criteria (horizontally) on the matrix.

5. Complete matrix by first rating all ideas against the first criterion, then rating ideas against the second criterion, and so forth. Ask, "If you (idea) will it (criteria)?" and place a smile, so-so, or frown face in the square.

Lesson 17

THE GAME OF ALoU

Purpose:
To focus on positively evaluating and giving feedback after playing a game using the ALoU tool.

Key Point:
Introduce a focusing tool called Advantages, Limitations, Overcoming Limitations, and Unique Qualities (ALoU). Positively evaluate a game-playing activity by pointing out the strong points, picking out areas for improvements, and discussing what's unique about the activity.

Materials & Preparation:
Focusing rules
Plus (+), minus (-), and star stamps, stickers, markers, or sponges to draw shapes
Ink pad
Strips of blank paper
Select a game or activity to play (i.e., Charades, Simon Says, Musical Chairs) and gather materials needed for the game.

Warm Up:

1. Explain to students how we'll play a game today and then learn a tool to help us figure out what we liked about the game, how we might play it better, and whether we'd like to play it again.

2. Students draw or stamp a vertical strip of pluses and talk about how pluses will tell us all the things we like about the game.

3. Students draw or stamp a vertical strip of minuses and explain how we'll be asked to point out what we don't like about the game. Minuses are for things that bug you.

4. Students draw or stamp a vertical strip of stars and explain how the game might stand out as different in our minds. Also, stars are about good things that might happen in the future as a result of our game.

5. Play the game.

Digging Deeper:

1. Explain that we want to think about whether we like the game or not. We'll start with the pluses first.

2. Draw a plus sign on large chart paper. Ask students to hold up their strip of pluses and share with a partner all of the pluses, good points, or advantages of the game.

3. Share the pluses in a large group and record on the chart paper under the plus sign.

4. Draw a minus sign on the chart paper. Ask students to hold up their strip of minuses and share with a partner all of the minuses, bad points, or limitations of the game.

5. Share the minuses as a large group. Help the students rephrase the limitations or minuses starting with "How to … ?" and record on chart paper.

6. Draw a star on the chart paper. Ask students to hold up their strip of stars and share with a partner all of the good things that might happen as a result of playing this game. Ask them to finish the sentence "It might …," "We might …," or "It is … ".

7. Share the stars as a large group and record on chart paper.

8. Give each student several dots and ask them to pick a couple of the biggest limitations listed.

9. Next, select one of the biggest limitations. Rewrite the "How to … ?" statement on a new sheet of chart paper. Have the students help you brainstorm ideas to solve the problem. Select a few and discuss how it helps to solve the problem.

Extension:

1. Debrief the learning: What did we do? How did you judge the game? What do the pluses, minuses, and stars mean? (Give examples for each.) Why did you tell me all the pluses first? How do the pluses make me feel? Why did we start the minuses with "How to … ?" How does the ALoU help us decide if the game is good? How does it help us make the game better? How does it help us decide whether we'd want to play it again?

Enhancements:

1. Use the ALoU to evaluate far out ideas, such as wacky party ideas or inventions.

2. Use the ALoU to evaluate student products before they are finished. Then, ask the students to improve the product based on the ALoU results.

ALoU

IDEA: ....

Advantages

+

Limitations (overcome)

- # How to

Unique Qualities

★

Lesson 18

DESIGNING A STUFFED ANIMAL ALoU

Purpose:

To focus on positive evaluation, strengthening, and development of a small number of options using ALoU.

Key Point:

Use the ALoU tool to focus and evaluate the designs for new stuffed animals.

Materials & Preparation:

ALoU Worksheet
Stuffed animal designs on Post-it® from Force a Stuffed Relationship lesson.
Draw a large ALoU worksheet on chart paper as the sample.

Warm Up:

1. Review focusing rules.

2. Display and discuss the new stuffed animal designs on Post-its®.

Digging Deeper:

1. Have the group of students select a design that is a "hit" for them and place the chosen Post-it® on the top of the large sample ALoU worksheet.

2. Discuss the advantages or pluses of the design and write them on the chart paper and on individual worksheets.

3. Discuss the limitations or minuses and write them starting with "How to … ?"

4. Discuss the unique qualities or star qualities and write them on the sheet.

5. Have students select and share a limitation to overcome. Brainstorm ideas to overcome it.

Extension:

1. Have each student or group of students present their design to the class by stating the +, -, or ★ of the design.

2. Debrief the learning: What did we do? How did you judge the design? Why did you look at the pluses first? Why did we start the minuses with "How to … ?" How does the ALoU help us decide if the design is good? How does it help us learn more about the design?

Enhancements:

Have students use a plus, minus, and star as a format for giving feedback anytime a classmate makes a presentation to the class or a new idea is presented.

Going Beyond an Introduction to ALoU

You can use the ALoU to evaluate and develop a small number of ideas or options. For example, here are some steps to follow when evaluating and developing some ideas using ALoU:

1. Review focusing rules.

2. Discuss and list the key data and ideas generated on chart paper.

3. Select up to three ideas to evaluate and develop further using the ALoU, and complete an ALoU on each separately. Complete steps 4–8 for each idea.

4. Generate all of the advantages of the idea. Ask students for the pluses of the idea.

5. Generate the limitations of the idea. Phrase the limitations "How to … ?" Ask students for the minuses of the idea.

6. Generate the unique qualities of the idea. Ask students, "What is new about it? What are the star qualities?"

7. Select the key limitations using hits.

8. Generate ideas to overcome key limitations, one at a time.

9. Once one to three ideas have been evaluated using the ALoU, compare the results and discuss which to carry forward.

APPENDIX

Appendix A: Adaptations of CPS Tools

	Manipulatives	Visual/Symbols	Semantic	Movement
All Generating Tools	**Generate Sign** • Hand-held green "Go" sign • Side one: word "Generate" • Side two: traffic light symbol for "Go"	**Symbols** • Green with picture of hands outstretched—all generating activities • Four symbols: — crossed-out gavel — many ideas on flip chart — imaginary creature — balloon to hot air balloon to airplane	**Simple Language** • Four generating guidelines: 1. Don't judge 2. Lots of ideas 3. Wild & crazy 4. Piggyback	**Move Whole Body** • Stretch out—all of your body, to illustrate physically the meaning of "generating."
All Focusing Tools	**Focus Sign** • Hand-held red "Stop" sign • Side one: word "Focus" • Side two: traffic light symbol for "Stop"	**Symbols** • Red with picture of closed-tight body—all focusing activities. • Four symbols: — smiling face — map — tools — product with price tag	**Simple Language** • Four focusing guidelines: 1. Be positive. 2. Look at "new." 3. Use your head. 4. Look where you're going.	**Move Whole Body** • Close your arms and hug your body tightly to illustrate physically the meaning of "focusing."

Generating Tools	Manipulatives	Visual/Symbols	Semantic	Movement
Brainstorming	**Post-it® Notes** • One idea per note • Write large with markers.	**Pictures** • Symbols to represent each guideline	**Poster** • Simplified language for all four generating guidelines.	**Action** • When using Post-its®, participants post their notes on the flip chart.
Braindrawing		**Worksheet** • Visual format for representing ideas by drawing them	**Poster** • Students draw their ideas (may add words to clarify, help recall).	
Forced Relationships	**Small Toys** • Twice as many toys as students for each group • Hold up toy to share ideas it suggests. **Character Stamps** • Stamp two figures. • Combine them into a new idea.	**Worksheet** • Visual containing blanks for addition number sentences • Character stamps are used as "addends." • New "forced fit" idea is used as the "sum."		**Costumes** • Act out a character or role in costume. • Force fit new ideas from your character's role.
Idea Checklists (SCAMPER)	**LEGO® toys or Blocks** • Build a structure. • Use idea checklist (e.g., SCAMPER words) to modify or improve the structure.	**Worksheet** • Visual with sections for each checklist word or phrase • Provide one space for new ideas that are suggested by each item in the checklist, (e.g., each SCAMPER word).	**Simple Language** • Use SCAMPER as example: *Substitute*–remove something, add something else; *Combine*–put two things together; *Adapt*–change; *Modify*–bigger/smaller; *Eliminate*–remove; *Rearrange*–change things around.	**Role Play** • Act out how each of the checklist words might be shown by a person or object. (Example: Act out something getting bigger, or smaller, or a character making a change, eliminating something, or making a substitution.)

Focusing Tools	Manipulatives	Visual/Symbols	Semantic	Movement
Hits	**Stickers** • Put your sticker on an idea that really sparkles.	**Poster** • Show ideas really "shining" or "lighting up."	**Simple Language** • An idea you really like • An idea that could help you solve the problem • Gets you excited about the idea	**Dots or Stickers** • Walk up to the flip chart to put your dots or stickers on the hits.
Highlighting	**Post-it® Notes** • Move the notes with hits on them into groups (ideas that belong together).	**Poster** • Ice cream cone as a symbol • Cone = problem • Scoops of ice cream= hot spots of ideas		**Dots or Stickers** • Put hits on index cards. • Sort them into groups that go together (hot spots).
ALoU	**Sponge Shapes** • Hold up a sponge (+, -, or ★) to show which part of ALoU is being worked on. • Use sponge shapes as stamps when doing individual ALoU.	**Symbols** • + for Advantages • - for Limitations (o = overcome) • ★ for Unique qualities	**Simple Language** • A = What's good? • L = What might be a wrong? (o = overcome) • U = What's new or different about it? It might …	
Matrix	**Vote Cards** • Hold up green, yellow, or red card to vote. **Face Stickers** • Place a happy face, so-sol face, or frowning face in matrix.	**Poster** • Matrix key includes: Yes: green, smiling face; Maybe: yellow, or neutral face; No: red, frowning face.		**Walk-In Matrix** • Use large mats or circles on floor, with faces or colors; step into the circle to vote.

Appendix B: References and Resources for CPS

Draze, D. (1986). *Primarily problem solving*. San Luis Obispo, CA: Dandy Lion Publications.

Duling, G. (1983). *CPS for the eency weency spider*. Buffalo, NY: DOK.

Duling, G. (1984). *CPS for the fourth little pig*. Buffalo, NY: DOK.

Eberle, B. (1996). *SCAMPER*. Waco, TX: Prufrock Press.

Eberle, B. (1996). *SCAMPER On!* Waco, TX: Prufrock Press.

Eberle, B., & Stanish, B. (1996). *CPS for kids*. Waco, TX: Prufrock Press.

Eberle, B., & Stanish, B. (1996). *Be a problem solver*. Waco, TX: Prufrock Press.

Ekvall, G. (1991). The organizational culture of idea-management: A creative climate for the management of ideas. In J. Henry & G. Walker (Eds)., *Managing innovation*. London: Sage.

Isaksen, S. I., Treffinger, D. J., and Dorval, K. B. (1994). *Creative approaches to problem solving*. Dubuque, IA: Kendall-Hunt.

Parnes, S. (Ed.). (1992). *Sourcebook for creative problem solving*. Buffalo, NY: Creative Education Foundation.

Puccio, K. (1994). *An analysis of an observational study of creative problem solving for primary children*. Unpublished master's thesis. Buffalo State College: Buffalo, NY.

Puccio, K., Keller-Mathers, S., & Treffinger, D. (2000). *Adventures in real problem solving: Facilitating creative problem solving with primary students*. Waco, TX: Prufrock Press.

Treffinger, D. (2000). *Practice problems for creative problem solving*. Waco, TX: Prufrock Press.

Treffinger, D. (1994). *The real problem solving handbook*. Sarasota, FL: Center for Creative Learning.

Treffinger, D., Isaksen, S., & Dorval, K. (2000). *Creative problem solving: An introduction*. Waco, TX: Prufrock Press.

Treffinger, D. (2000). *Creative problem solver's guidebook.*. Waco, TX: Prufrock Press.

Treffinger, D. (2000). *Assessing CPS performance*. Waco, TX: Prufrock Press.